ANSEL
1991 Engagement Calendar

Little, Brown and Company

Bulfinch Press

Boston · Toronto · London

Cover: Moon and Half Dome, Yosemite National Park, California, 1960

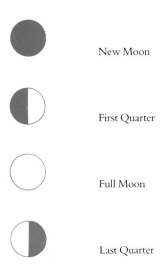

New Moon

First Quarter

Full Moon

Last Quarter

Copyright © 1990 by the Trustees of The Ansel Adams Publishing Rights Trust.
All rights reserved. No part of this calendar may be reproduced in any form or by any electronic or mechanical means, including information storage and retrieval systems, without permission in writing from the publisher.

ISBN 0-8212-1792-5

Bulfinch Press is an imprint and trademark of Little, Brown and Company (Inc.)
Published simultaneously in Canada by Little, Brown & Company (Canada) Limited

Designed and composed at Meriden-Stinehour Press
Printed by Gardner Lithograph

PRINTED IN THE UNITED STATES OF AMERICA

Ansel Adams

There is something very satisfying about the thought that within ten feet of you at any given time lies enough material to keep you busy a lifetime learning to understand it. And I don't mean *interpretations* of things, or predetermined convictions about things. I really feel like Stieglitz who would lie against a rock all day and photograph the clouds that came overhead with a small Graflex. He did hundreds of them — calls them "Equivalents" — and they are swell. They are all small contact prints and have tremendous impact. He called them "Equivalents" because, for him, they represented moods — they were *equivalent* to something felt deep within. Really now — isn't practically everything that we react to just that?

—from a letter to Cedric Wright, July 13, 1940,
Ansel Adams: Letters and Images 1916–1984

Clearing Winter Storm, Yosemite National Park, California, 1944

Trees in Snow, Glacier Point Road, Yosemite National Park, California, 1962

Sunrise, Mount Tom, Sierra Nevada, California, 1948

Redwood Tree, Mariposa Grove, Winter, Yosemite National Park, California, c. 1937

Half Dome, Apple Orchard, Winter, Yosemite National Park, California, c. 1935

Mount Robson, Jasper National Park, Canada, 1928

Frozen Lake and Cliffs, Sierra Nevada, Sequoia National Park, California, 1932

Sentinel Rock and Clouds, Winter, Yosemite National Park, California, c. 1937

Evening Cloud, Ellery Lake, Sierra Nevada, California, 1934

Moon and Clouds, Northern California, 1959

Surf, Big Sur Coast, California, c. 1980

Rocks, Bakers Beach, San Francisco, California, c. 1932

Rock and Surf, Monterey County Coast, California, c. 1951

Rushing Water, Merced River, Yosemite National Park, California, c. 1955

Trailside, near Juneau, Alaska, 1948

Tenaya Creek, Dogwood, Rain, Yosemite National Park, California, c. 1948

Dogwood, Yosemite National Park, California, c. 1938

Orchard, Early Spring, Portola Valley, California, c. 1940

Starr King Fall from Base, Yosemite National Park, California, c. 1940

Nevada Fall, Yosemite National Park, California, c. 1946

Yosemite Falls, Azaleas, Yosemite National Park, California, c. 1940

Child in Mountain Meadow, Yosemite National Park, California, c. 1943

Eggs in Nest, Yosemite National Park, California, c. 1936

Leaves, Mount Rainier National Park, Washington, c. 1942

Deer, Yosemite National Park, California, c. 1935

Forest, Early Morning, Mount Rainier National Park, Washington, 1949

Mount Clarence King, Pool, Kings Canyon National Park, California, c. 1925

Stream, Sea, Clouds, Rodeo Lagoon, Marin County, California, 1962

Tenaya Lake, Mount Conness, Yosemite National Park, California, c. 1946

Old Faithful Geyser, Yellowstone National Park, Wyoming, 1942

Ghost Ranch Hills, Chama Valley, New Mexico, 1937

Evening Clouds and Pool, East Side of the Sierra Nevada, from the Owens Valley, California, c. 1962

Sand Dunes, Sunrise, Death Valley National Monument, California, c. 1948

Organ Pipe Cactus National Monument, Arizona, c. 1952

Sequoia Gigantea Roots, Yosemite National Park, California, c. 1950

Pipes and Gauges, Charlestown, West Virginia, 1939

Dawn, Autumn, Great Smoky Mountains National Park, Tennessee, 1948

Half Dome, Autumn, Yosemite National Park, California, 1938

Forest and Stream, Northern California, 1959

Poplars, Autumn, Owens Valley, California, c. 1937

The Black Sun, Owens Valley, California, c. 1939

Gate, Nambe Road, near Pojoaque, New Mexico, 1972

White House Ruin, Canyon de Chelly National Monument, Arizona, 1942

Autumn Storm, Los Trampas, near Peñasco, New Mexico, c. 1958

Arches, North Court, Mission San Xavier del Bac, Tucson, Arizona, 1968

Evening Cloud, Sierra Nevada, California, 1936

Clearing Storm, Sonoma County Hills, California, 1951

Winter Sunrise, Sierra Nevada, from Lone Pine, California, 1944

Trees, near Washburn Point, Yosemite National Park, California, c. 1945

Moon and Half Dome, Yosemite National Park, California, 1960

Fresh Snow, Yosemite National Park, California, c. 1947

Half Dome, Merced River, Winter, Yosemite National Park, California, c. 1938

Pine Forest in Snow, Yosemite National Park, California, 1933

1991

JANUARY
S	M	T	W	T	F	S
		1	2	3	4	5
6	7	8	9	10	11	12
13	14	15	16	17	18	19
20	21	22	23	24	25	26
27	28	29	30	31		

FEBRUARY
S	M	T	W	T	F	S
					1	2
3	4	5	6	7	8	9
10	11	12	13	14	15	16
17	18	19	20	21	22	23
24	25	26	27	28		

MARCH
S	M	T	W	T	F	S
					1	2
3	4	5	6	7	8	9
10	11	12	13	14	15	16
17	18	19	20	21	22	23
24	25	26	27	28	29	30
31						

APRIL
S	M	T	W	T	F	S
	1	2	3	4	5	6
7	8	9	10	11	12	13
14	15	16	17	18	19	20
21	22	23	24	25	26	27
28	29	30				

MAY
S	M	T	W	T	F	S
			1	2	3	4
5	6	7	8	9	10	11
12	13	14	15	16	17	18
19	20	21	22	23	24	25
26	27	28	29	30	31	

JUNE
S	M	T	W	T	F	S
						1
2	3	4	5	6	7	8
9	10	11	12	13	14	15
16	17	18	19	20	21	22
23	24	25	26	27	28	29
30						

JULY
S	M	T	W	T	F	S
	1	2	3	4	5	6
7	8	9	10	11	12	13
14	15	16	17	18	19	20
21	22	23	24	25	26	27
28	29	30	31			

AUGUST
S	M	T	W	T	F	S
				1	2	3
4	5	6	7	8	9	10
11	12	13	14	15	16	17
18	19	20	21	22	23	24
25	26	27	28	29	30	31

SEPTEMBER
S	M	T	W	T	F	S
1	2	3	4	5	6	7
8	9	10	11	12	13	14
15	16	17	18	19	20	21
22	23	24	25	26	27	28
29	30					

OCTOBER
S	M	T	W	T	F	S
		1	2	3	4	5
6	7	8	9	10	11	12
13	14	15	16	17	18	19
20	21	22	23	24	25	26
27	28	29	30	31		

NOVEMBER
S	M	T	W	T	F	S
					1	2
3	4	5	6	7	8	9
10	11	12	13	14	15	16
17	18	19	20	21	22	23
24	25	26	27	28	29	30

DECEMBER
S	M	T	W	T	F	S
1	2	3	4	5	6	7
8	9	10	11	12	13	14
15	16	17	18	19	20	21
22	23	24	25	26	27	28
29	30	31				

1992

JANUARY
S	M	T	W	T	F	S
			1	2	3	4
5	6	7	8	9	10	11
12	13	14	15	16	17	18
19	20	21	22	23	24	25
26	27	28	29	30	31	

FEBRUARY
S	M	T	W	T	F	S
						1
2	3	4	5	6	7	8
9	10	11	12	13	14	15
16	17	18	19	20	21	22
23	24	25	26	27	28	29

MARCH
S	M	T	W	T	F	S
1	2	3	4	5	6	7
8	9	10	11	12	13	14
15	16	17	18	19	20	21
22	23	24	25	26	27	28
29	30	31				

APRIL
S	M	T	W	T	F	S
			1	2	3	4
5	6	7	8	9	10	11
12	13	14	15	16	17	18
19	20	21	22	23	24	25
26	27	28	29	30		

MAY
S	M	T	W	T	F	S
					1	2
3	4	5	6	7	8	9
10	11	12	13	14	15	16
17	18	19	20	21	22	23
24	25	26	27	28	29	30
31						

JUNE
S	M	T	W	T	F	S
	1	2	3	4	5	6
7	8	9	10	11	12	13
14	15	16	17	18	19	20
21	22	23	24	25	26	27
28	29	30				

JULY
S	M	T	W	T	F	S
			1	2	3	4
5	6	7	8	9	10	11
12	13	14	15	16	17	18
19	20	21	22	23	24	25
26	27	28	29	30	31	

AUGUST
S	M	T	W	T	F	S
						1
2	3	4	5	6	7	8
9	10	11	12	13	14	15
16	17	18	19	20	21	22
23	24	25	26	27	28	29
30	31					

SEPTEMBER
S	M	T	W	T	F	S
		1	2	3	4	5
6	7	8	9	10	11	12
13	14	15	16	17	18	19
20	21	22	23	24	25	26
27	28	29	30			

OCTOBER
S	M	T	W	T	F	S
				1	2	3
4	5	6	7	8	9	10
11	12	13	14	15	16	17
18	19	20	21	22	23	24
25	26	27	28	29	30	31

NOVEMBER
S	M	T	W	T	F	S
1	2	3	4	5	6	7
8	9	10	11	12	13	14
15	16	17	18	19	20	21
22	23	24	25	26	27	28
29	30					

DECEMBER
S	M	T	W	T	F	S
		1	2	3	4	5
6	7	8	9	10	11	12
13	14	15	16	17	18	19
20	21	22	23	24	25	26
27	28	29	30	31		

Posters by Ansel Adams

The finest quality reproductions on heavy coated paper, suitable for framing

Old Faithful Geyser

Sand Dunes, Sunrise

Mount McKinley Range, Clouds

Aspens (vertical)

El Capitan, Winter, Sunrise

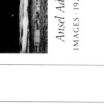
The Tetons and the Snake River

Frozen Lake and Cliffs

Oak Tree, Snowstorm

Moonrise

Mount McKinley and Wonder Lake

Winter Sunrise

The Golden Gate before the Bridge

Leaves

Clearing Winter Storm

Mount Williamson

Aspens (horizontal)

Moon and Half Dome

Monolith, The Face of Half Dome

Order Form

SHIP TO

Name _____ Daytime telephone _____

Address _____

City _____ State _____ Zip _____

Please provide street address rather than post office box number as all shipments will be via United Parcel Service.

QUANTITY		PRICE	AMOUNT
	Books by Ansel Adams		
_____	The American Wilderness — Cloth (0–8212–1799–2)	$100.00	$_____
_____	Ansel Adams: An Autobiography — Cloth (0–8212–1596–5)	$60.00	$_____
_____	— Paper (0–8212–1787–9)	$29.45	$_____
_____	Ansel Adams: Classic Images — Cloth (0–8212–1629–5)	$29.45	$_____
_____	Ansel Adams: Letters and Images 1916–1984 — Cloth (0–8212–1691–0)	$50.00	$_____
_____	— Paper (0–8212–1788–7)	$29.45	$_____
_____	Examples: The Making of 40 Photographs — Cloth (0–8212–1551–5)	$44.00	$_____
_____	— Paper (0–8212–1750–X)	$27.00	$_____
_____	Photographs of the Southwest — Cloth (0–8212–0699–0)	$60.00	$_____
_____	— Paper (0–8212–1574–4)	$34.00	$_____
_____	The Portfolios of Ansel Adams — Cloth (0–8212–0723–7)	$45.00	$_____
_____	— Paper (0–8212–1122–6)	$24.50	$_____
_____	Singular Images — Paper (0–8212–0728–8)	$18.45	$_____
_____	Yosemite and the Range of Light — Cloth (0–8212–0750–4)	$150.00	$_____
_____	— Paper (0–8212–1523–X)	$29.45	$_____
	The Ansel Adams Photography Series		
_____	The Camera / Book 1 — Cloth (0–8212–1092–0)	$27.00	$_____
_____	The Negative / Book 2 — Cloth (0–8212–1131–5)	$27.00	$_____
_____	The Print / Book 3 — Cloth (0–8212–1526–4)	$27.00	$_____
	Posters by Ansel Adams		
_____	Aspens (horizontal) (0–8212–1742–9)	$25.00	$_____
_____	Aspens (vertical) (0–8212–1498–5)	$25.00	$_____
_____	Clearing Winter Storm (0–8212–1496–9)	$25.00	$_____
_____	El Capitan, Winter, Sunrise (0–8212–1743–7)	$25.00	$_____
_____	Frozen Lake and Cliffs (0–8212–1532–9)	$25.00	$_____

continued on overleaf

	The Golden Gate before the Bridge (0–8212–1654–6)	$25.00	$_____
_____	The Golden Gate before the Bridge (0–8212–1654–6)	$25.00	$_____
_____	Leaves (0–8212–1567–1)	$25.00	$_____
_____	Monolith, The Face of Half Dome (0–8212–1531–0)	$25.00	$_____
_____	Moon and Half Dome (0–8212–1592–2)	$25.00	$_____
_____	Moonrise (0–8212–1134–X)	$25.00	$_____
_____	Mount McKinley and Wonder Lake (0–8212–1591–4)	$25.00	$_____
_____	Mount McKinley Range, Clouds (0–8212–1790–9)	$25.00	$_____
_____	Mount Williamson (0–8212–1566–3)	$25.00	$_____
_____	Oak Tree, Snowstorm (0–8212–1568–X)	$25.00	$_____
_____	Old Faithful Geyser (0–8212–1694–5)	$25.00	$_____
_____	Sand Dunes, Sunrise (0–8212–1590–6)	$25.00	$_____
_____	The Tetons and the Snake River (0–8212–1693–7)	$25.00	$_____
_____	Winter Sunrise (0–8212–1533–7)	$25.00	$_____

Calendars by Ansel Adams

_____	Ansel Adams 1991 Wall Calendar (0–8212–1791–7)	$14.95	$_____
_____	Ansel Adams 1991 Engagement Calendar (0–8212–1792–5)	$12.95	$_____
		Subtotal	$_____
	California, Massachusetts, and New York residents must include sales tax*		$_____
		Total	$_____

☐ I enclose check/money order payable to Little, Brown and Company for the total due above. Publisher pays postage and handling.

OR

Charge my ☐ American Express ☐ Visa ☐ MasterCard. $1.50 for one item, and $.50 for each additional item ordered, will be charged for postage and handling.

Account number ☐☐☐☐ ☐☐☐☐ ☐☐☐☐ ☐☐☐☐

Expiration date _____ Signature _____

*CA — 6%; MA — 5%; NY — 4%; NYC — 8.25%

Prices shown on this order form are current prices and are subject to change without notice.

Send orders to: Little, Brown and Company
Fulfillment Center
200 West Street
P.O. Box 902
Waltham, MA 02254–9961
Or call toll-free: 1–800–343–9204

ALSO AVAILABLE AT BOOKSTORES